ESCAPE ROOM PUZZLES

ESCAPE THE Space Station!

An Interactive Puzzle Adventure

Written by Em Bruce

Illustrated by Lilia Miceli

ARCTURUS

Welcome to Escape the Space Station!

Congratulations! You've won a huge worldwide contest to visit the Orbital Space Laboratory, where Earth's greatest scientists are performing out-of-this-world experiments in the utmost secrecy. You can't believe your luck, especially since you've heard that there are those who would do anything to get a sneak preview of the O.S.L.'s amazing discoveries.

In just a few minutes, you'll blast off on your journey to the O.S.L., but who knows what you'll encounter when you arrive? You'll need all your wits, courage, and puzzle-solving skills—not to mention the odd helpful robot—to navigate your way through the challenges that await you. So sit back, strap in, and get ready to take one giant leap into the unknown ...

From the office of the Orbital Space Laboratory

GROUND CONTROL OFFICER: Artemis Tereshkova
HEADQUARTERS: Confidential
SUBJECT: International O.S.L. Contest

Congratulations, we are pleased to inform you that you have been chosen as the winner of the international contest to visit the Orbital Space Laboratory. Please present yourself at the Armstrong Space Academy at 2:00 pm sharp on the third Saturday of this month for your preflight medical checks and g-force training. Further instructions to follow.

We look forward to welcoming you onboard the O.S.L.

Commander Nova Darwish

Nova Darwish

How to read this book

In this book—just like in space—things work a little differently. You won't be reading this one from front to back. You must find your own route through the book to solve the mysteries. Each puzzle will have three or four possible solutions.
When you think you know the correct one, turn to the entry indicated in the text and see if you're right. Use your skills of observation, lateral thinking, and logic to uncover clues and solve the mysteries. The illustrations are packed with information, so keep your eyes peeled!

Difficulty levels:

Choose your difficulty level, then race against the clock to solve the mystery!

CLUE-COLLECTING CADET: You have two-and-a-half hours to solve all the puzzles. You also have five lives, which means that you're allowed to get the answers wrong up to four times.

PUZZLE-SOLVING PILOT: You have two hours to solve all the puzzles and just four lives. Get more than three answers wrong, and you have to start again!

CODE-CRACKING COMMANDER: You have just one-and-a-half hours to solve all the puzzles and three lives, so you can't afford to make any mistakes!

Symbol code:

The crew of the O.S.L. come from all over the world, so they often use a symbol code to make sure important information doesn't get lost in translation. This table will help you decode it.

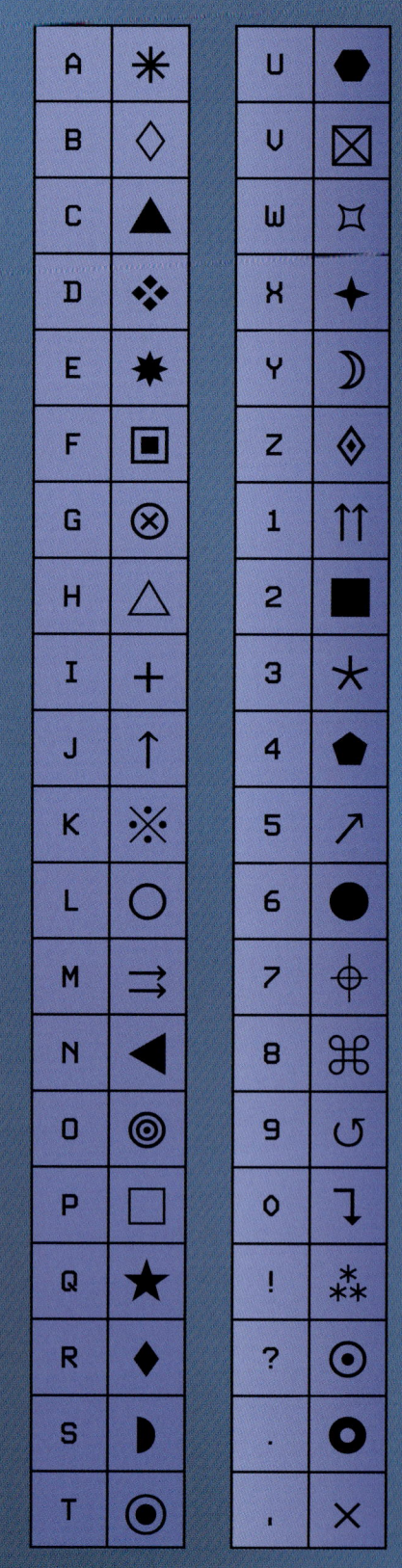

Letter/number code:

Use this table to decode messages or clues where numbers are substituted for letters, or vice versa.

A	B	C	D	E	F	G	H	I	J	K	L	M
1	2	3	4	5	6	7	8	9	10	11	12	13

N	O	P	Q	R	S	T	U	V	W	X	Y	Z
14	15	16	17	18	19	20	21	22	23	24	25	26

.	,	!	?	;	:	-	'
27	28	29	30	31	32	33	34

Dot code:

Another universal code that the crew of the O.S.L. uses is this dot code. It substitutes letters for dots. You can use this table to get your head around it.

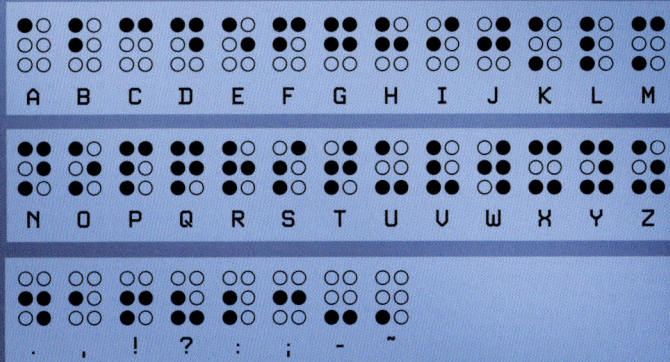

Map of the O.S.L.:

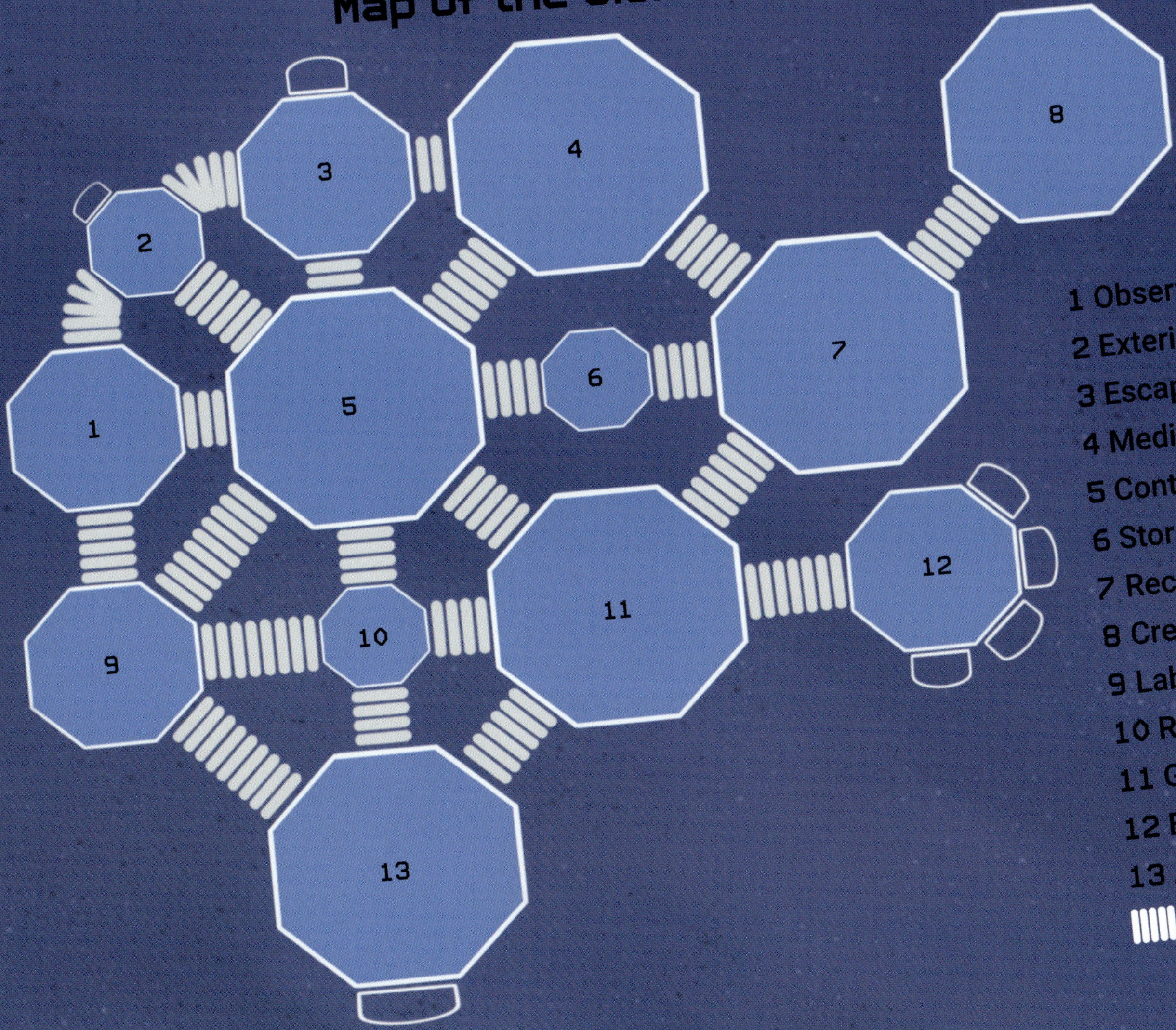

1 Observation deck
2 Exterior hatch
3 Escape pod
4 Medical bay
5 Control room
6 Storage bay
7 Recreation bay
8 Crew's quarters
9 Laboratory
10 Recycling pod
11 Galley
12 External docks
13 Atrium
|||| Access tunnels

1 Launch day is finally here! You're strapped into the tiny transport capsule, ready for liftoff. But before you have a chance to pinch yourself, a screen suddenly flickers into life on the avionics deck.

Good afternoon, CAPSULE-1, this is Commander Nova Darwish. We look forward to welcoming you on board the O.S.L.—if you can find your way here, that is. I'm sure I left something in there that'll help you figure out the launch sequence. Over.

USE THIS RULE

START WITH STARS, THEN IT'S MARS. END WITH ROVER, THEN START OVER.

Trace a line from the top row of buttons to the launch button. You can move up, down, left or right but not diagonally. Which button do you press first?

Button A1, turn to entry 208.
Button C1, turn to entry 59.
Button E1, turn to entry 82.

2 I'm afraid that's not quite right. Untangle your way back to entry 150.

3 That's not Commander Darwish's supply box. Close it carefully, then return to entry 136.

4 Nope, it wasn't in the medical bay. Head back to entry 205.

5 That's the one! You grab some wire cutters and wrench open the electrical panel to find ... an impossible tangle of wires! The alarms are blaring, and MAL's eerily calm voice echoes across the PA system: "5 ... 4 ... 3 ...." It's now or never if you want to disable the manual override!

Hands trembling, you cut wire ...

... A, turn to entry 30.
... B, turn to entry 159.
... C, turn to entry 135.
... D, turn to entry 194.

6 You won't make it in time going this way! Sprint back to entry 100.

7 I'm afraid that's not quite right. Make your way back to entry 43.

8 Nothing good awaits you in this tunnel! Carefully tiptoe back to entry 202.

9

At least that's one robot back online! Fox leaves to deliver the supply boxes from the capsule and tells you to swing by the medical bay for a checkup before meeting him and the other astronauts in the lab. He gives you a map of the O.S.L. to help you find your way around.

To get to the lab via the medical bay,
you take route ...

... A, go to entry 143.
... B, go to entry 186.
... C, go to entry 74.

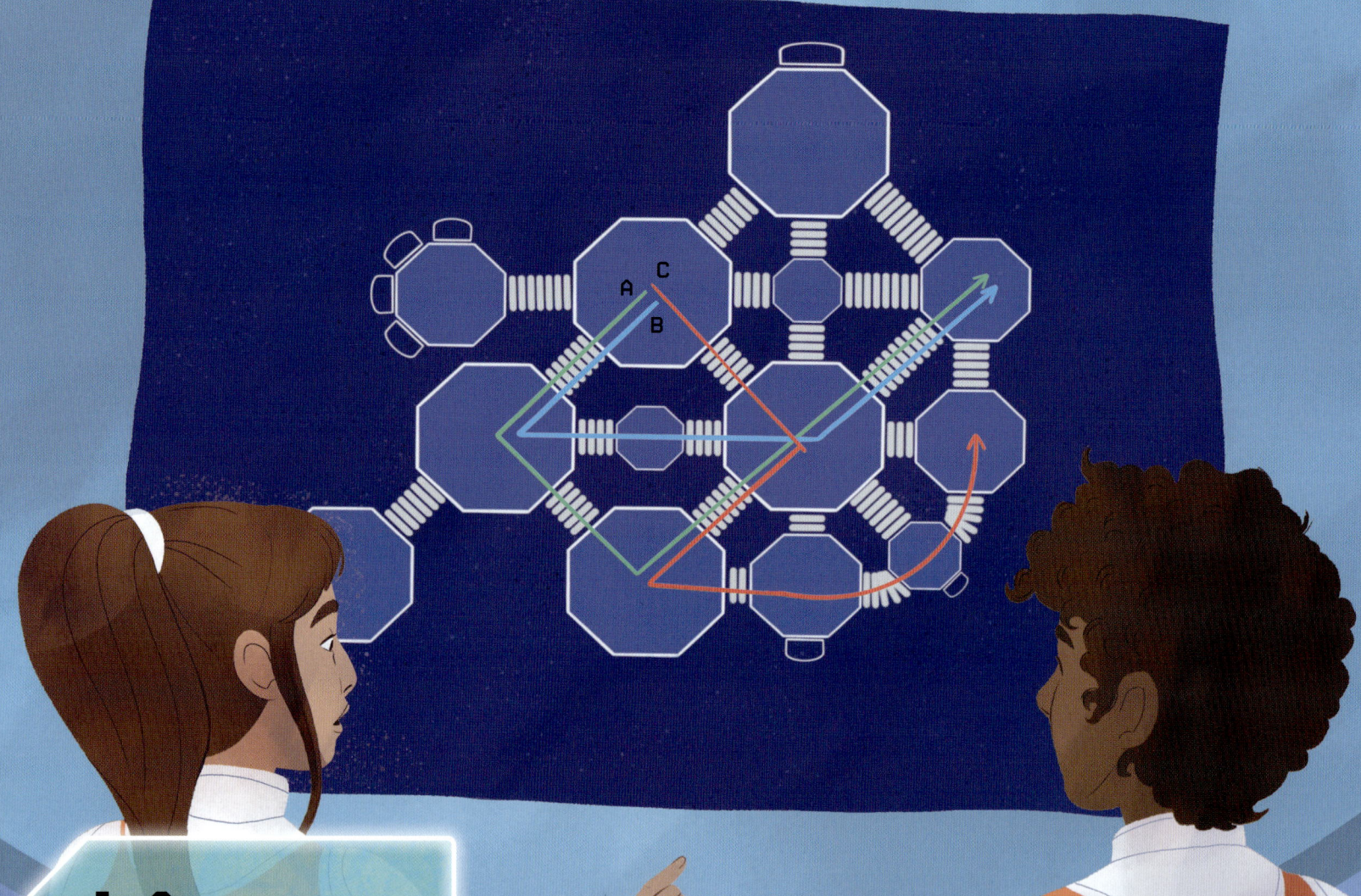

10
Your Klixanovian needs some work! *Flerb* back to entry 156, and try again.

11
No, zeplium isn't in the IUED. Make your way back to entry 184.

12
No, you definitely do need that part! Put it back carefully, and return to entry 93.

13 The tubes release you, and you walk through the recreation bay. The crew's quarters are just a few steps ahead of you, but so is MAL! A sprawling web of high-powered, thermo-vaporizing lasers covers the ground.

You realize your only option is to …

… try to step carefully through the lasers, go to entry 58.
… turn back and use another route, go to entry 188.
… turn off your gravity boots, go to entry 122.

14 That attachment won't fit the release mechanism. Turn back to entry 166.

15 No, Commander Darwish is still there. Head back to entry 30, and look again.

16

The hatch clunks open loudly. Finally, you step foot inside the O.S.L.! A man is waiting to greet you; he introduces himself as Science Officer Castor Fox and hands you four key cards.

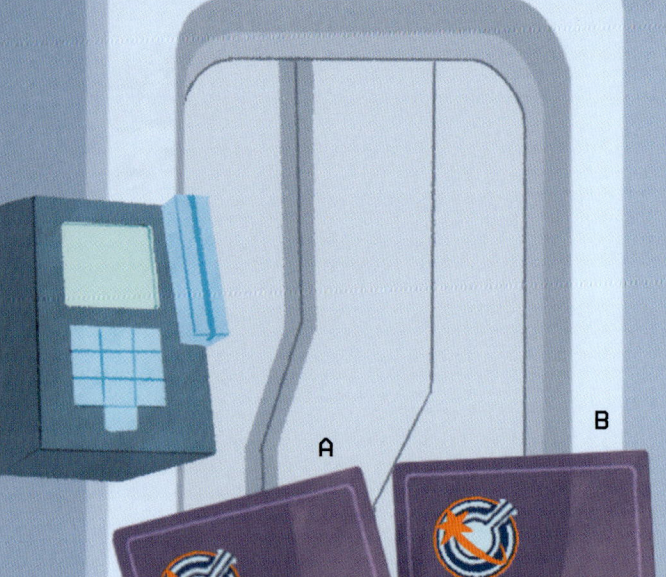

"I'M AFRAID MAL—OUR ONBOARD A.I.—IS A LITTLE GLITCHY TODAY. I ASKED IT TO PRINT YOU AN ACCESS CARD SO YOU CAN GET AROUND THE O.S.L., BUT I'M PRETTY SURE ONLY ONE OF THESE IS GENUINE."

You examine the key cards closely and choose …

… A, go to entry 155.
… B, go to entry 90.
… C, go to entry 192.
… D, go to entry 60.

17
That's not the correct reboot code word. Puzzle your way back to entry 72.

18
Impact! Impact! Quickly steer back to entry 177.

19 You know just what to do: You run back to the galley to find the helper robot you fixed earlier. You insert the odd-shaped memory card, and the robot hums to life. It's asking for a passcode, which you don't have, but maybe you can figure it out?

You enter the passcode ...

... H1P4L, go to entry 52.
... H0WD1, go to entry 129.
... H3LL0, go to entry 172.
... H1Y42, go to entry 83.

20 That's not the code to restart the stabilizer. Float back to entry 76, and try again.

21 That's not the code to open the fuel valve. Head back to entry 57.

22 That's not what the message is about. Head back to entry 97 for another try.

23 Backpack full, you make your way out of the mines and back to the O.S.L. You decide to take a different route to avoid Geyser Grove, but you wander into a patch of carnivorous plants! You're quickly ensnared by one of them, and it begins to pull you closer to the snapping mouth of the main stem. Perhaps if you cut the main stem at the base, the plant will let you go.

You pull out your scissors and cut stem ...

... A, go to entry 78.
... B, go to entry 57.
... C, go to entry 131.

24 That's not quite right, I'm afraid. Track back to entry 195, and try again.

25 No, the book isn't in that section. Put it back, and return to entry 37.

26 I'm afraid that's not what Commander Darwish's message says. Head back to entry 129.

30 Phew! That was way too close! While MAL reboots, you run to the lab to see if the effects of the hypersleep essence have worn off, but all the astronauts are still floating around fast asleep. Or are they?

You notice that the person missing from the lab is …

… Science Officer Ohsumi, go to entry 91.
… Commander Darwish, go to entry 15.
… Science Officer Aldrin, go to entry 75.
… Science Officer Fox, go to entry 198.

31 I'm afraid that's not quite right. Make your way back to entry 43.

32 I'm afraid that's not quite right. Untangle your way back to entry 150.

33

That's right, a bottle of hypersleep essence is missing. Dr. Wong accompanies you to the lab, where you finally meet Commander Darwish and her crew. She explains that the O.S.L. is powered by a small black hole, but they need a more reliable fuel source. Their experiments have narrowed it down to four possible elements, and she says that if you can find out what they are, you can join in the experiments.

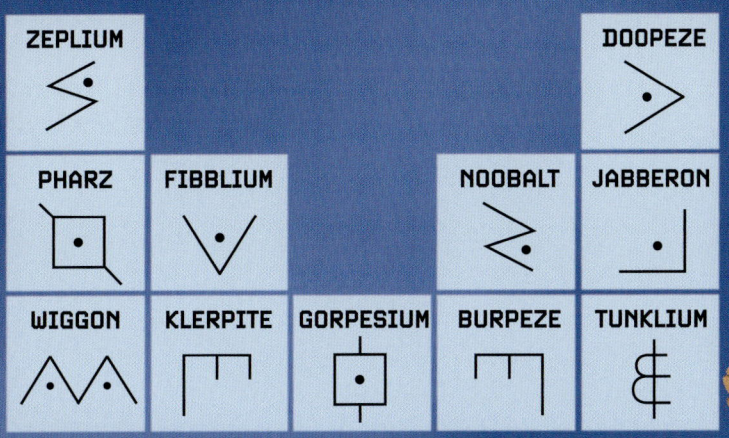

You identify the four elements as …

… pharz, wiggon, jabberon, and fibblium, go to entry 39.

… doopeze, noobalt, gorpesium, and wiggon, go to entry 190.

… burpeze, tunklium, zeplium, and klerpite, go to entry 121.

… jabberon, zeplium, pharz, and klerpite, go to entry 184.

34
That's not the right air duct! Brew some more antidote, and head back to entry 68.

35
Those coordinates won't get you to the O.S.L. Navigate back to entry 40.

36
That's not the code to open the escape pod door. Escape back to entry 170.

37

That's right, only 15 minutes until the sun rises and melts the sealant keeping the O.S.L.'s hull together! It's time to call in the professionals—you need to wake the crew. You race back to the medical bay and find Dr. Wong's medical textbooks, but which one might reveal the hypersleep antidote? HAN-D1 recalls that Dr. Wong gave him a clue to find the right book in case she was ever incapacitated.

> IT CONTAINS ALL THE VOWELS, SIX LETTERS OCCUR TWICE EACH, AND TWO LETTERS OCCUR THREE TIMES.

A
- ALGERNON'S ALIEN ANATOMY
- WHAT GOES UP: DIGESTION IN ZERO GRAVITY VOL. 1
- Let's Look Closely at Space Blindness

B
- SLEEP IT OFF: RESTING IN SPACE
- MUST COME DOWN: DIGESTION IN ZERO GRAVITY VOL. 2
- Big Bangs: Bumps, Bruises, and Breaks in Space

C
- Dr. Singe's Handbook of Potions, Lotions, and Balms
- Callisto's Complete Text of Intergalactic Ills

D
- PERCHANCE TO DREAM: A COMPLETE GUIDE
- Dr. Deimos' Directory of Astro Ailments

You think carefully and find the book you need in section …

… A, go to entry 25.
… B, go to entry 132.
… C, go to entry 119.
… D, go to entry 110.

38
That's not the right constellation. Stargaze your way back to entry 82.

39
I'm afraid those aren't the right elements. Check the chart again back at entry 33.

40

Nice astronomy skills! You orient the capsule in the direction of Hoppa, but you know you'll need exact coordinates to reach the O.S.L. You think about what Commander Darwish said, "We keep the secrets of the O.S.L. hidden in the stars …"

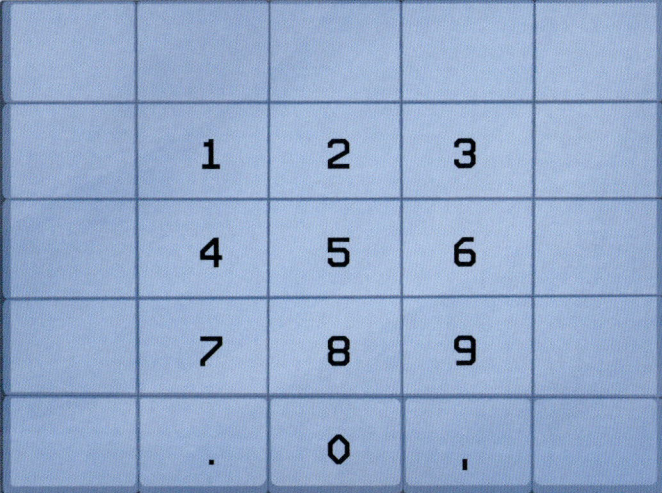

TIP: WHAT IF THE LETTERS OF HOPPA WERE NUMBERS?

After checking your letter/number substitution code, you enter the coordinates …

… 82.11, 81.61, go to entry 204.
… 81.83, 16.17, go to entry 35.
… 81.51, 61.61, go to entry 177.
… 88.41, 12.19, go to entry 138.

41
That combination won't open the hatch. Dial your way back to entry 61.

42
No, you won't find axtris cocoyum there! Head back to entry 174.

43

Good job! Fox isn't going anywhere with that zeplium sample now! But that's where the good news ends ... MAL announces that the black hole that powers the station became unstable during the reboot. The stabilizer needs to be turned back on, but it's on the outside of the O.S.L. Unfortunately, MAL can only remember the first half of the sequence to open the exterior hatch: 60, 50, 41, 33, 26.

You figure out that the rest of the sequence is ...

... 24, 16, 11, 9, 5, go to entry 109.

... 21, 17, 14, 12, 11, go to entry 7.

... 19, 13, 8, 4, 2, go to entry 31.

... 20, 15, 11, 8, 6, go to entry 160.

44
I'm afraid that's not the correct answer. Take a closer look back at entry 163.

45
That's not the right air duct! Brew some more antidote, and head back to entry 68.

46
That's not the right concoction. Hurry back to entry 110— time is running out!

47 That's right! Suddenly, you hear a rustling behind you and turn to see a group of aliens watching you intently. You're not sure if you should be worried, but fortunately, HAN-D1 is a member of the intergalactic social network, Spacebook. He pulls up the profiles of the four closest matches on your tablet.

MALLOVEANS:
Like: Fungi, sharp sticks, and mousetraps.
Dislike: Fluffy blankets.
Status: Venomous, do not approach.

EGNOGISH:
Like: Painting, hiking, and eggnog.
Dislike: Flying snakes.
Status: Twinned with Pingonia.

PINGONIANS:
Like: Recorder music, marshmallows, and gardening.
Dislike: Volcano monsters.
Status: It's complicated

KLIXANOVIANS:
Like: Puzzles and rainy days.
Dislike: Geysers.
Status: Looking for friends.

You work out that you must be on …

… Klixanovia, go to entry 156.
… Mallovea, go to entry 51.
… Pingonia, go to entry 206.
… Egnog, go to entry 165.

48 You won't find the entrance to the zeplium mine there. Recalculate, and return to entry 79.

49 That's not what the message is about. Head back to entry 97 for another try.

50

With klerpite no longer in the running, Science Officer Stella Aldrin asks you to help her compare the combustibility of the remaining elements with some dark matter from the black hole that powers the O.S.L. She explains that the new fuel source has to be at least twice as combustible as the dark matter, but it can't be more than four times as combustible.

DARK MATTER   PHARZ   ZEPLIUM   JABBERON

COSMIC COMBUSTOMETER

0   9   18   27   36

NOT COMBUSTIBLE — VERY COMBUSTIBLE

You carefully add the combustion compound and rule out …

… pharz, go to entry 54.
… zeplium, go to entry 112.
… jabberon, go to entry 163.

51
No, you're not on Mallovea. Find your way back to entry 47, and try again.

52
I'm afraid that's not the robot's passcode. Make your way back to entry 19.

53 Good job! This is definitely Commander Darwish's cabin. But now you're stumped; where's the reboot code word? You turn over her message and realize there's more on the back. At first, it doesn't make sense, but then you wonder if only one letter in each word needs to make sense …

> NEPTUNE EASILY WINS SPARKLIEST PLANET, ALTHOUGH PLUTO'S EQUALLY RADIANT.

You decipher the message and reach for …

… the newspaper, go to entry 72.
… the book, go to entry 154.
… the photo, go to entry 162.

54 Pharz was the wrong element to rule out. Find your way back to entry 50.

55 That circuit board won't work. Do the robot all the way back to entry 191.

56 That's not the correct reboot code word. Puzzle your way back to entry 72.

57

Phew! You cut the right stem and wriggle free of the snapping plant. Panting and sweating, you arrive back at the stranded O.S.L., where HAN-D1 has fixed the broken sensor dish. Now you just need to get the external fuel valve open, and you can finally get out of here! In the reboot, the fuel valve code switched from a numerical code to an alphabetical one, but luckily MAL remembers how he came up with it.

TIP: THIS LOOKS LIKE A JOB FOR THE LETTER/NUMBER SUBSTITUTION CODE!

$7 \times 3 =$

$19 - 5 =$

$6 + 13 =$

$15 \div 3 =$

$8 \div 8 =$

$3 \times 4 =$

1	R	Y	J	T	Z
2	G	M	F	U	C
3	B	O	W	D	S
4	V	L	P	H	K
5	E	Q	A	N	I

You key in the code …

… UNLOCK, go to entry 21.

… UNSHUT, go to entry 203.

… UNBOLT, go to entry 148.

… UNSEAL, go to entry 174.

58
There's no way you can step through those lasers! Take your singed toes back to entry 13.

59
Oops, that's not the correct launch sequence. The only place you're going is back to entry 1!

60
I'm afraid that's a fake key card. Swipe your way back to entry 16.

61

Docking complete! The outer hatch hisses loudly as it swings into the air lock. Instantly, you can feel your gravity boots taking effect. At the end of the air lock is a hatch leading to the O.S.L., secured with a rotary combination lock. You fish a final clue out of your envelope from Commander Darwish.

After you enter the combination, the arrow is pointing to the symbol …

…◇◇, go to entry 199.
…8, go to entry 41.
…△, go to entry 16.
…✳, go to entry 127.

62
No, I'm afraid that's not the right gravity level. Bounce back to entry 180, and try again.

63
No, that's not how long you have until the sun rises. Try once more back at entry 140.

64
That's not the code name for the manual override. Zip back to entry 187.

65

Now you just need to input O.S.L.'s original location. The only problem is that unlike the transport capsule, the O.S.L.'s navigation system only uses the onboard symbol code.

TIP: YOU'LL NEED THE O.S.L.'S LOCATION FROM ENTRY 82.

ENTER LOCATION

You enter the combination …

… △ + □ □ ◎, go to entry 171.

… △ ◎ □ □ ✻, go to entry 118.

… △ ◎ ◎ □ ◗, go to entry 85.

66
That attachment won't fit the release mechanism. Turn back to entry 166.

67
I'm afraid that's not the right time. Rewind back to entry 118.

68

That's the one! You race to the control room to distribute the solution into the ventilation system. You pause when you reach the O.S.L.'s complex system of air ducts. You can only empty the hypersleep antidote into one of them, but which one?

VEGA

LYRA

TIP: YOU'LL NEED THE FLIGHT SYSTEMS CODE NAMES FROM ENTRY 187.

ANTARES

SIRIUS

You cross your fingers and empty the solution down the duct named …

… Vega, go to entry 45.
… Lyra, go to entry 108.
… Antares, go to entry 34.
… Sirius, go to entry 97.

69
I'm afraid that's not the answer to the riddle. Head back to entry 90, and try again.

70
That's not Commander Darwish's cabin. Close the door, and return to entry 122.

71
No, I'm afraid you don't have that long! Hurry back to entry 125.

72

That's gotta be it! You open the newspaper and flick through it. You're not sure what you're looking for, but you stop when you reach the puzzle pages. It looks like Commander Darwish has left some clues for you in the sudoku.

Fill the empty squares so that the numbers 1–9 appear once in each row, column, and minigrid.

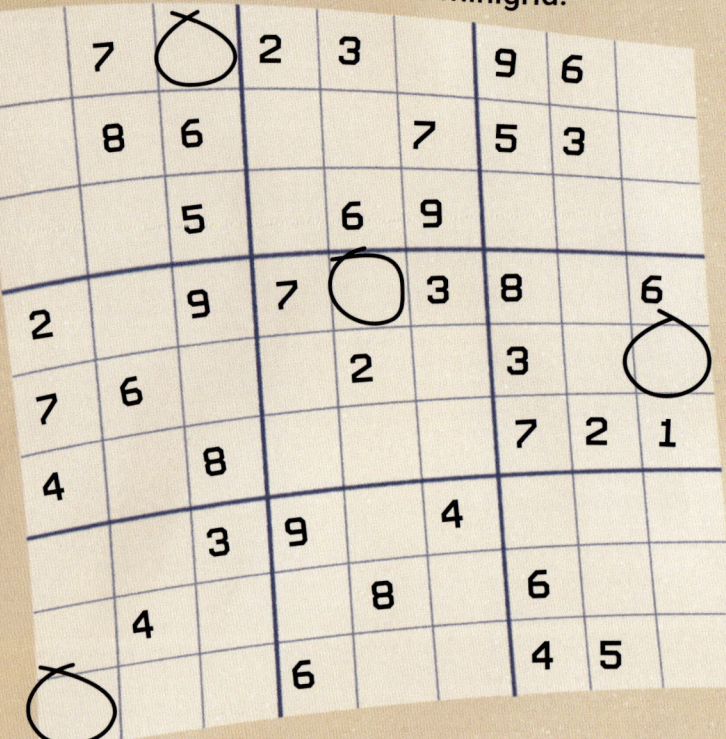

You complete the sudoku and use the letter/substitution code to find the code word ...

... EACH, go to entry 56.
... IDEA, go to entry 161.
... HEAD, go to entry 100.
... HIDE, go to entry 17.

73

Nope, that docking station isn't compatible. Back up to entry 153.

74

That route won't get you there. Retrace your steps back to entry 9.

75

No, Science Officer Aldrin is still there. Head back to entry 30, and look again.

76

You'd better get a move on! When you reach the damaged stabilizer, you find that it's been sabotaged! MAL tells you that it's too late to stabilize the black hole completely. Your only option is to force it to form a wormhole! Use the code word ORBIT to initiate the emergency protocol.

You enter the code ...

⠕⠗⠃⠊⠞, go to entry 152.

⠉⠕⠙⠑⠎, go to entry 20.

⠎⠞⠁⠗⠞, go to entry 180.

⠏⠕⠺⠑⠗, go to entry 201.

77
That's not your safety tether. Quick, float back to entry 160 while you still can!

78
That's not the main stem! Try again at entry 23.

79 That's right, it's zeplium. And you're in luck, because the aliens have a zeplium mine! They show you a map—but rather than tell you the coordinates of the entrance, the mischievous creatures want you to solve a riddle. The first part of the coordinates is a letter that is six letters from the first letter of the volcano's name. The second part is the answer to 15 x 4 divided by the answer to 27 − 15.

You head in the direction of grid point ...

... K7, go to entry 48.
... S5, go to entry 133.
... O4, go to entry 179.

80 I'm afraid that's not what Commander Darwish's message says. Head back to entry 129.

81 That's not the geyser-free route! Take your singed eyebrows back to entry 133.

82

That must be the correct launch sequence because the capsule suddenly thunders into life. You can barely hear Commander Darwish over the roar of the powerful engines.

> CAPSULE-1, YOU HAVE LIFTOFF. NOW, THE LOCATION OF THE O.S.L. IS CLASSIFIED, BUT I'VE LEFT YOU AN ENVELOPE OF CLUES TO HELP YOU FIND US. ALL I'LL SAY IS THAT WE KEEP THE SECRETS OF THE O.S.L. HIDDEN IN THE STARS. OVER.

HOPPA

LAZIUS MINOR

SQUIRRELEUS MAJOR

TENTACULA

You open the envelope to find a star map and the first clue. You realize Commander Darwish has sketched the constellation …

… Tentacula, go to entry 38.

… Lazius Minor, go to entry 137.

… Squirreleus Major, go to entry 145.

… Hoppa, go to entry 40.

83
I'm afraid that's not the robot's passcode. Make your way back to entry 19.

84
I'm afraid that's not the answer to the riddle. Head back to entry 90, and try again.

85
That's not quite the right code. Take another look back at entry 65.

86

The door clunks open, and inside you find a very annoyed-looking Castor Fox. You did it! You saved the O.S.L. and its crew, stopped the treacherous Fox from escaping, and discovered a massive source of zeplium—and some new friends—on Klixanovia. Commander Darwish is thrilled and invites you to come back to the O.S.L. again next summer. Will that visit go a little more smoothly? Watch this space …

THE END

87 That's not the answer to the number riddle. Calculate your way back to entry 147.

88 That's not Commander Darwish's supply box. Close it carefully, then return to entry 136.

89 No, that's not what's missing from Dr. Wong's supplies. Take a closer look back at entry 143.

90

That's the one! You scan the key card, and the light on the door turns green—but it doesn't open. Suddenly, a calm, automated voice echoes through the speakers.

> THOUGHT YOU COULD JUST WALTZ INTO MY STATION, DID YOU? JUST AS WELL I ADDED A NUMBER CODE TO THIS DOOR. IF YOU CAN ANSWER THIS RIDDLE, YOU MIGHT BE ABLE TO WORK IT OUT: PEOPLE HAVE VISITED ME, BUT NOT MANY. I NEVER STAY FULL FOR LONG. I HAVE A DARK SIDE. WHAT AM I?

You think carefully, then using your letter/number substitution code you enter the code …

… 22, 15, 9, 4, go to entry 69.
… 13, 15, 15, 14, go to entry 191.
… 3, 1, 22, 5, go to entry 84.

91

No, Science Officer Ohsumi is still there. Head back to entry 30, and look again.

92

That's not the answer to the number riddle. Calculate your way back to entry 147.

93 Good job—your gravity boots are correctly calibrated! But there's bad news, too. As you step outside, MAL tells you that the journey through the wormhole has used up all the O.S.L.'s fuel and smashed one of the sensor dishes. HAN-D1 finds some spare pieces in the storage pod. Can you repair the broken dish using the other one as a guide?

You realize you don't need part ...

... B, go to entry 124.

... D, go to entry 193.

... E, go to entry 47.

... G, go to entry 12.

94 That's not the right amount of zeplium. Take your backpack back to entry 114.

95 That's not the code to open the escape pod door. Escape back to entry 170.

96 That's not Commander Darwish's supply box. Close it carefully, then return to entry 136.

97 You did it! You sprint to the lab and arrive in time to see the astronauts waking up. You fill them in on everything that happened, and Aldrin and Ohsumi rush to fix the tear in the hull. Commander Darwish can't believe that Castor Fox would betray them. You ask MAL to bring up Fox's most recent communication from Earth.

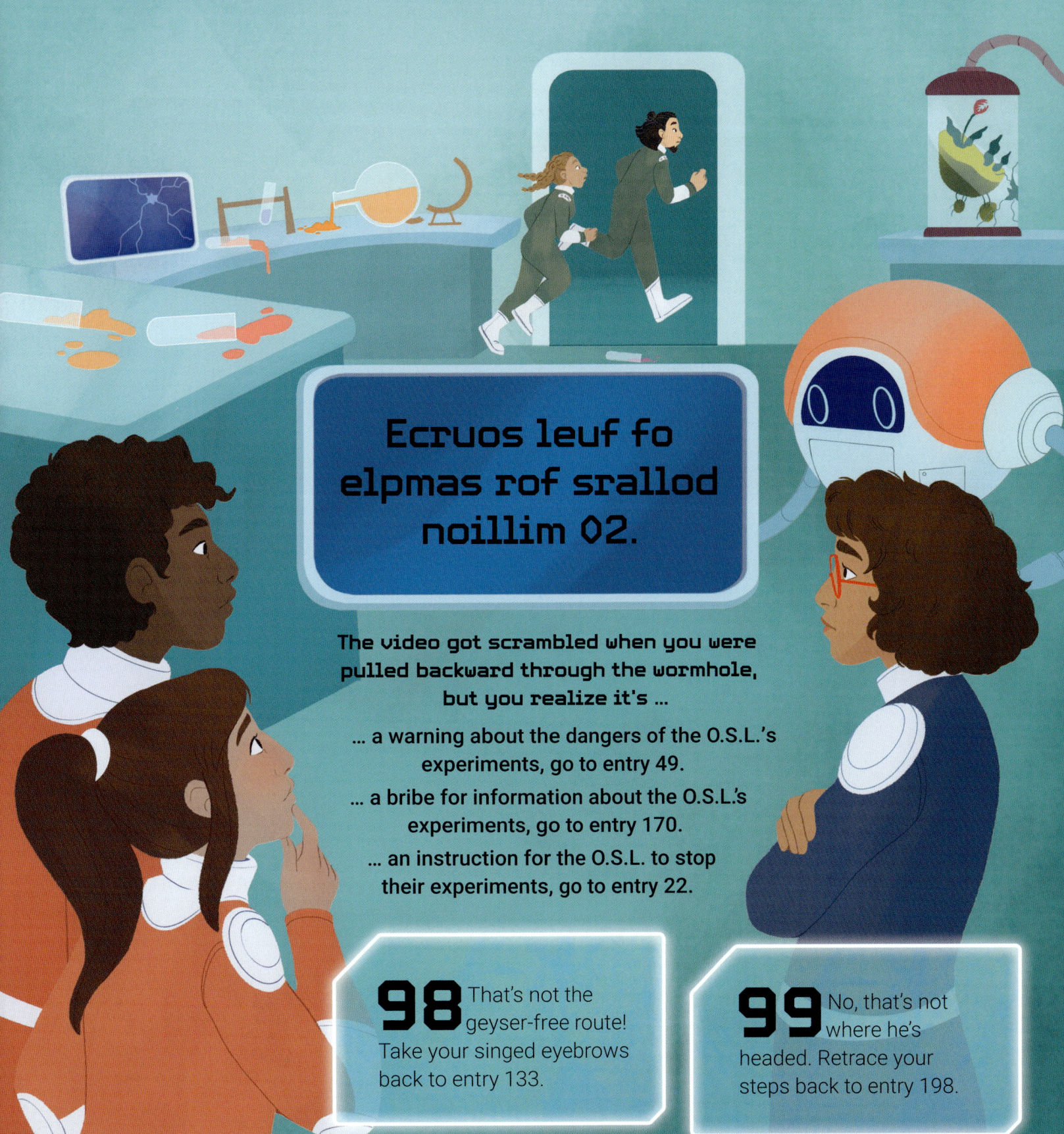

> Ecruos leuf fo elpmas rof srallod noillim 02.

The video got scrambled when you were pulled backward through the wormhole, but you realize it's …

… a warning about the dangers of the O.S.L.'s experiments, go to entry 49.

… a bribe for information about the O.S.L.'s experiments, go to entry 170.

… an instruction for the O.S.L. to stop their experiments, go to entry 22.

98 That's not the geyser-free route! Take your singed eyebrows back to entry 133.

99 No, that's not where he's headed. Retrace your steps back to entry 198.

100

Good job! You leave Commander Darwish's cabin and head back to the access tunnel—which is now laser-free. Phew! You're about to step in when MAL's voice booms out over the PA system. "Well, this has been fun, but I have my orders. Initiating O.S.L. self-destruct sequence in two minutes." You'd better get to the control room, fast! Hands trembling, you pull out your map and notice a handy key you hadn't spotted earlier.

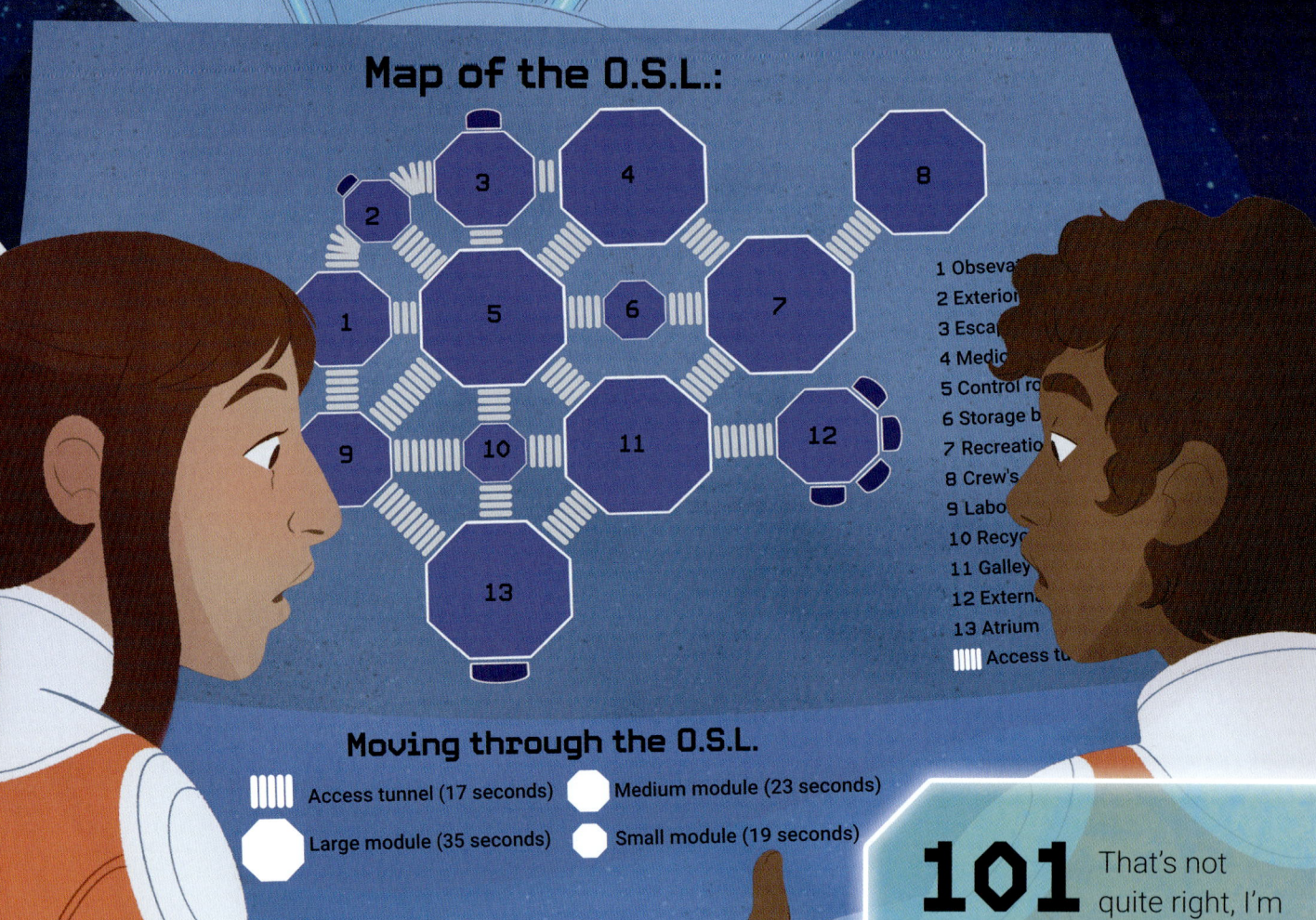

Map of the O.S.L.:

1 Obseva[tion]
2 Exterior
3 Esca[pe]
4 Medic[al]
5 Control ro[om]
6 Storage b[ay]
7 Recreatio[n]
8 Crew's
9 Labo[ratory]
10 Recyc[ling]
11 Galley
12 Extern[al]
13 Atrium
||||| Access tu[nnel]

Moving through the O.S.L.

- Access tunnel (17 seconds)
- Large module (35 seconds)
- Medium module (23 seconds)
- Small module (19 seconds)

The only route that will get you to the control room in time is via ...

... the medical bay, go to entry 151.
... the galley, go to entry 6.
... the recycling pod, go to entry 113.
... the storage bay, go to entry 187.

101
That's not quite right, I'm afraid. Track back to entry 195, and try again.

102
Nope, that docking station isn't compatible. Back up to entry 153.

103

You grab the emergency chocolate from Dr. Wong's supply box and give it to your new Klixanovian friends. You say your goodbyes and clamber on board the O.S.L. The only problem is you have no idea how to generate a new wormhole to get back home! You find a notebook in Darwish's cabin, but the page you need has been ripped up.

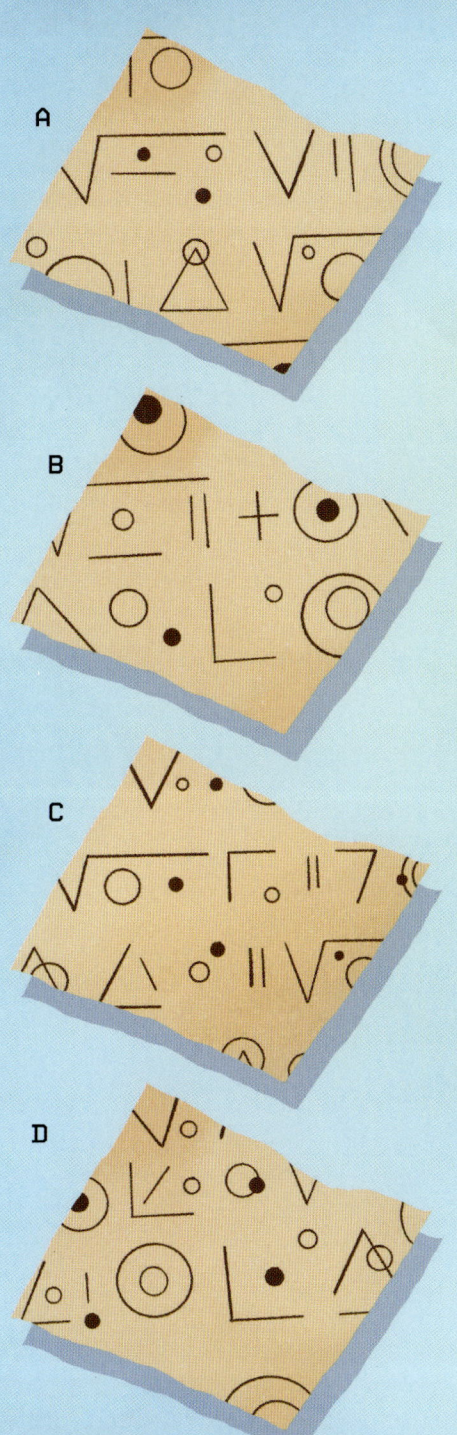

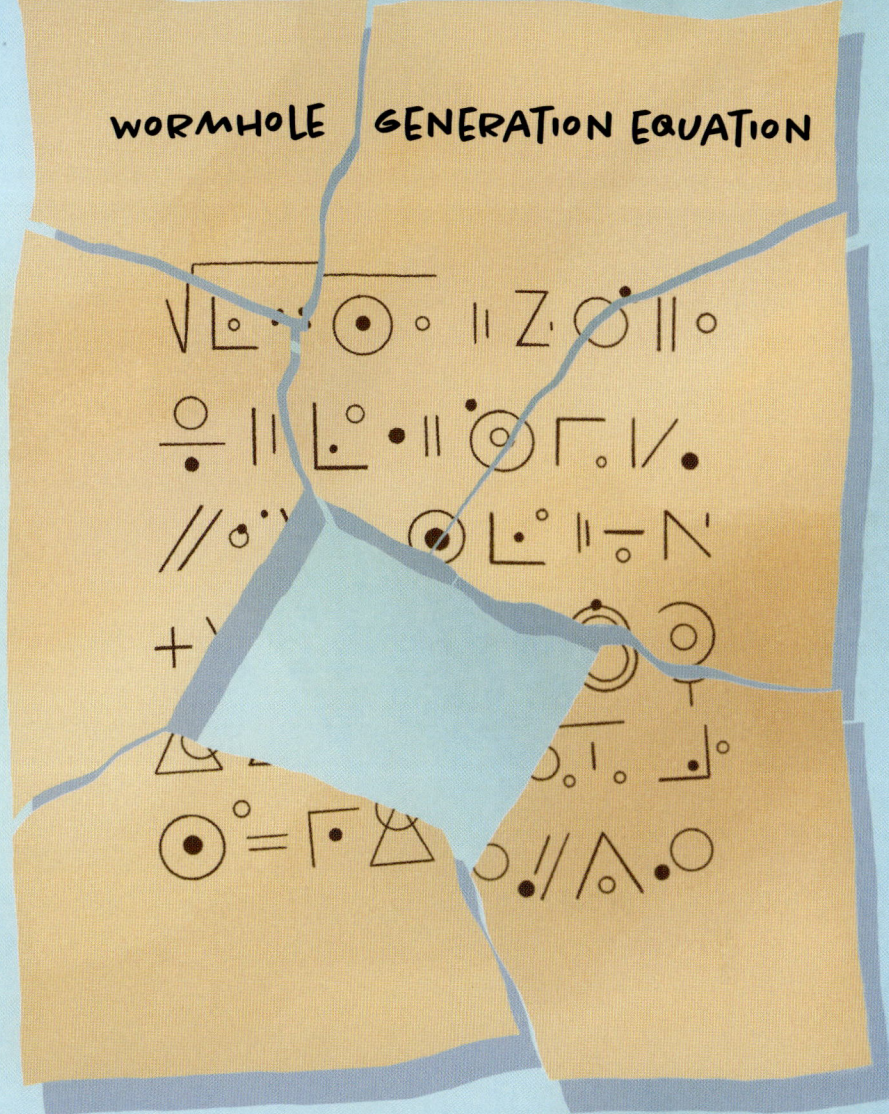

After putting the pieces back together, you work out that the final piece of the page is …

… A, go to entry 207.
… B, go to entry 175.
… C, go to entry 65.
… D, go to entry 28.

104 That's not Commander Darwish's cabin. Close the door, and return to entry 122.

105 That's not the right concoction. Hurry back to entry 110—time is about to run out!

106 I'm afraid that's not the right time. Rewind back to entry 118.

107

Impressive piloting! You make it safely through the belt, but a small piece of space junk knocked the docking probe offline—you can't dock with the O.S.L. without it! You go to turn it back on, but in all the jostling, the labels have fallen off the avionics deck. Panicking, you rifle through the envelope of clues, and you find something that might just help.

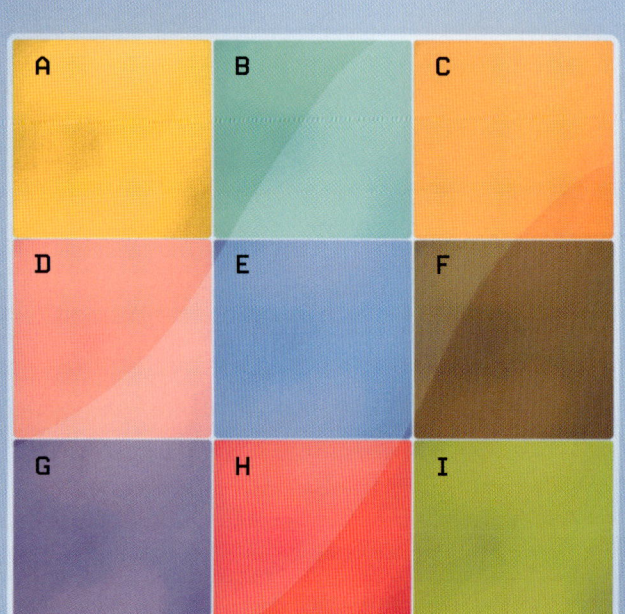

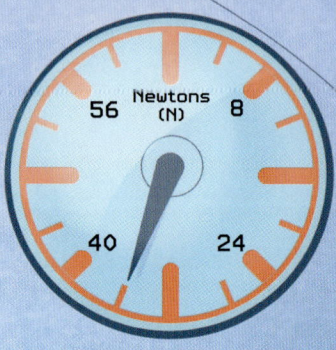

GRAVITY COUNTER

THE VERTICAL STABILIZER BUTTON IS TO THE LEFT OF THE DOCKING PROBE BUTTON.
THE TOP RIGHT BUTTON HAS NO FUNCTION.
THE BUTTONS FOR ENGINES 1, 2, AND 3 ARE IN A DIAGONAL LINE.
THE DOCKING PROBE BUTTON HAS NOTHING BELOW IT.

To reactivate the docking probe, you hit button …

… H, go to entry 136.
… E, go to entry 168.
… I, go to entry 116.

108
That's not the right air duct! Brew some more antidote, and head back to entry 68.

109
I'm afraid that's not quite right. Make your way back to entry 43.

110

That's the one! You flick through *Perchance to Dream: A Complete Guide* until you find the chapter on hypersleep. There's a recipe for an antidote, and all the ingredients you need are in Dr. Wong's medical bay. You grab some test tubes, and try to follow the instructions, but they're complicated. One of these concoctions is right, but which one?

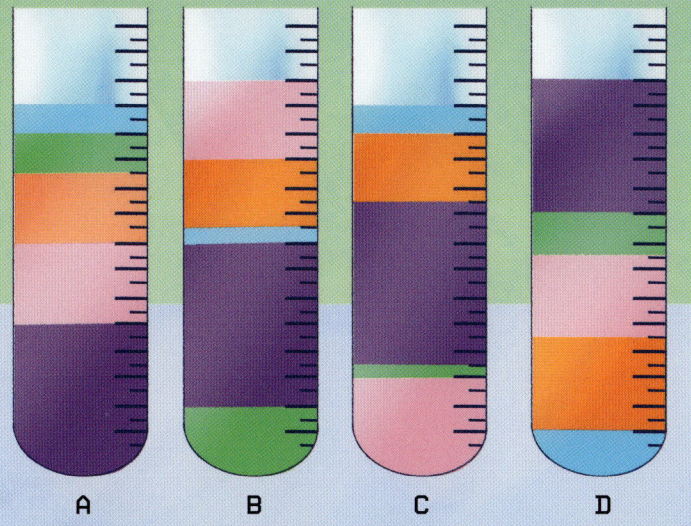

You check the textbook again and reach for test tube …

… A, go to entry 105.
… B, go to entry 46.
… C, go to entry 68.
… D, go to entry 164.

Hypersleep antidote:
One part perkz
Three parts arizium
Two and a half parts of alarmite
Twice as much wakiwakium as arizium
Half as much crowon as perkz

111
No, that's not what's missing from Dr. Wong's supplies. Take a closer look back at entry 143.

112
Zeplium was the wrong element to rule out. Find your way back to entry 50.

113
You won't make it in time going this way! Sprint back to entry 100.

114

Nice work! You make your way through the dark, damp tunnel and arrive at an enormous underground mine, full of sparkling zeplium. You open up your backpack and pause—exactly how much zeplium should you take? You don't want to take more than you need. Luckily, HAN-D1 gave you some instructions.

> The O.S.L.'s tank holds 8,000 galactic gallons of fuel, and it can't launch unless the tank is full.
>
> Each cosmic gram of zeplium converts to 20 gallons of fuel.

You fill up your backpack with exactly ...

... 200 cosmic grams of zeplium, go to entry 181.

... 240 cosmic grams of zeplium, go to entry 94.

... 400 cosmic grams of zeplium, go to entry 23.

115
I'm afraid that's not the right time. Rewind back to entry 118.

116
Oops, that's not the docking probe button! Probe your way back to entry 107.

117
No, you won't find axtris cocoyum there! Head back to entry 174.

118

You look out the window ... you can see Earth in the distance. You made it! You check your watch; you were on Klixanovia for 38 Earth minutes. However, MAL reminds you that time moves twice as fast on Klixanovia as it does on Earth. If it was 9:36 p.m on both planets when you landed, what time is it now in Earth time?

You set your watch from Klixanovian time to the Earth time of ...

... 10:52 p.m., go to entry 115.
... 10:14 p.m., go to entry 125.
... 9:55 p.m., go to entry 106.
... 9:36 p.m., go to entry 67.

119 No, the book isn't in that section. Put it back, and return to entry 37.

120 No, that's not what's missing from Dr. Wong's supplies. Take a closer look back at entry 143.

121 I'm afraid those aren't the right elements. Check the chart again back at entry 33.

122

Talk about thinking on your feet! You switch off your gravity boots and float carefully over the web of lasers. You switch your boots back on in time to land safely in front of the crew's quarters, but which cabin belongs to Commander Darwish? You'd better be quick, who knows what MAL will cook up next?

TIP: TAKE A CLOSER LOOK AT COMMANDER DARWISH'S MESSAGE FROM ENTRY 129.

You push the button to open door ...

... A, go to entry 53.
... B, go to entry 130.
... C, go to entry 104.
... D, go to entry 70.

123
That's not quite right, I'm afraid. Track back to entry 195, and try again.

124
No, you definitely do need that part! Put it back carefully, and return to entry 93.

125

That's right, it's now 10:14 p.m.. With a jolt of panic, you remember that the sealant you used to close the tear in the O.S.L.'s hull will melt as soon as the sun rises. You run back to the exterior hatch to check the countdown clock, but wormhole travel clearly didn't agree with it, and it's hanging from the wires. You need to know how long you have until sunrise.

TIP: TIME TO REVISIT THE CLOCKS FROM ENTRY 43?

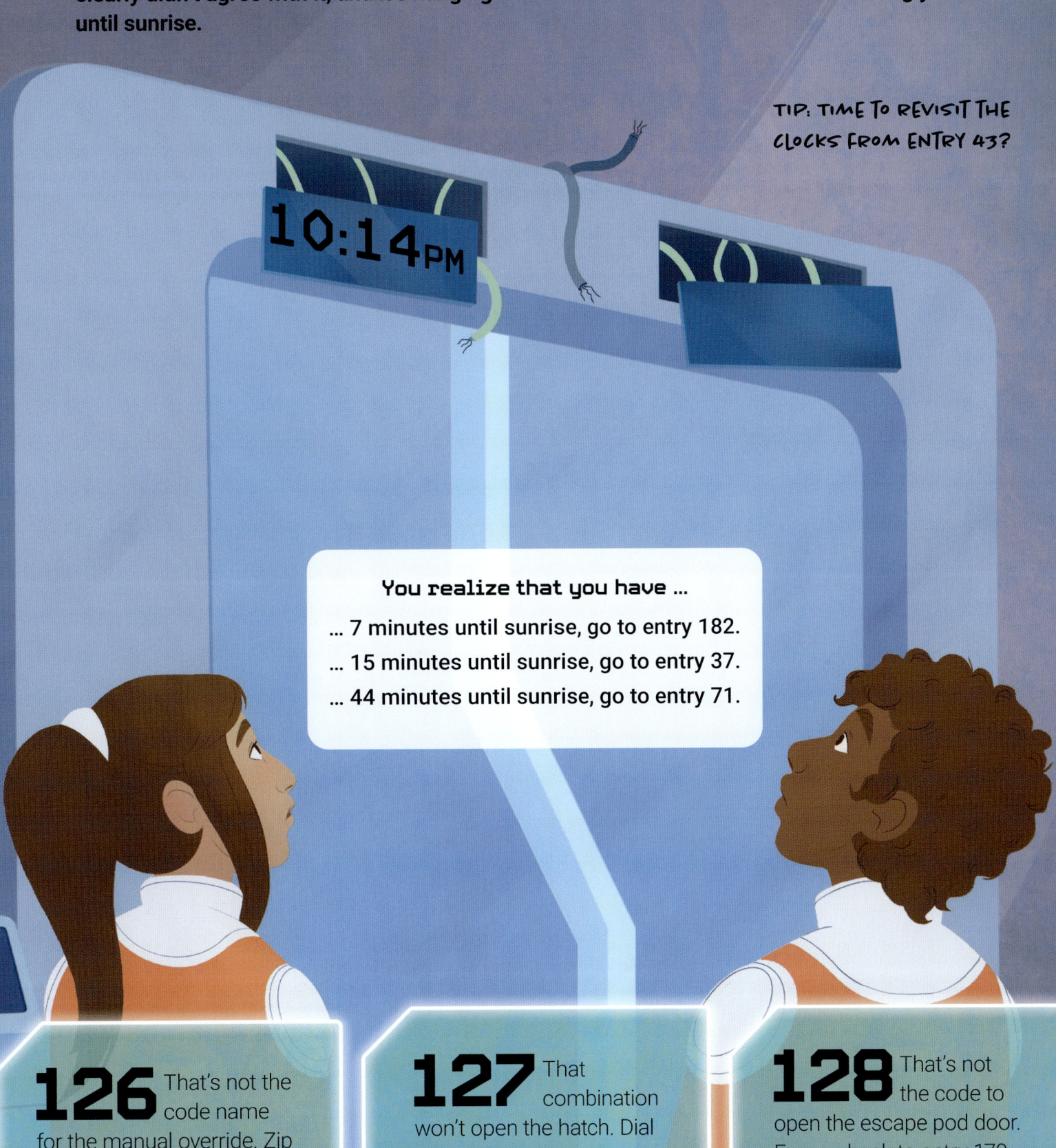

You realize that you have ...

... 7 minutes until sunrise, go to entry 182.

... 15 minutes until sunrise, go to entry 37.

... 44 minutes until sunrise, go to entry 71.

126
That's not the code name for the manual override. Zip back to entry 187.

127
That combination won't open the hatch. Dial your way back to entry 61.

128
That's not the code to open the escape pod door. Escape back to entry 170.

129

Good job! The robot begins to speak. "Hello. I am HAN-D1, your helper robot. I have a message for you from Commander Darwish." A message starts to print from HAN-D1's chest, but it's all in code! Luckily, you've seen this code before ...

You decode Commander Darwish's message. It suggests ...

... she released the hypersleep essence herself, go to entry 80.

... you should get MAL to help you escape, go to entry 26.

... she suspects MAL has been compromised, go to entry 150.

130
That's not Commander Darwish's cabin. Close the door, and return to entry 122.

131
That's not the main stem! Take another turn back at entry 23.

132
No, the book isn't in that section. Put it back, and return to entry 37.

133

You leave HAN-D1 behind to fix the sensor dish and make your way to the zeplium mine. After a while, you arrive at Geyser Grove. There's no way around it, so you have to go through it—but tread carefully!

You take a deep breath and follow route …

… A, go to entry 98.
… B, go to entry 81.
… C, go to entry 146.
… D, go to entry 202.

134
No, that's not where he's headed. Retrace your steps back to entry 198.

135
That's not the right wire! Nip back to entry 5 to try again.

136

The docking probe comes back online and not a minute too soon, since you can see the O.S.L. out of the window. Your heart starts to race, just as the screen crackles back into life. The message reads: "You're not far now CAPSULE-1. Before you board, you'll need to gear up. You can find special gravity boots in my supply box, but don't touch any of the other boxes."

You open up supply box …

… A, go to entry 3.
… B, go to entry 96.
… C, go to entry 27.
… D, go to entry 88.

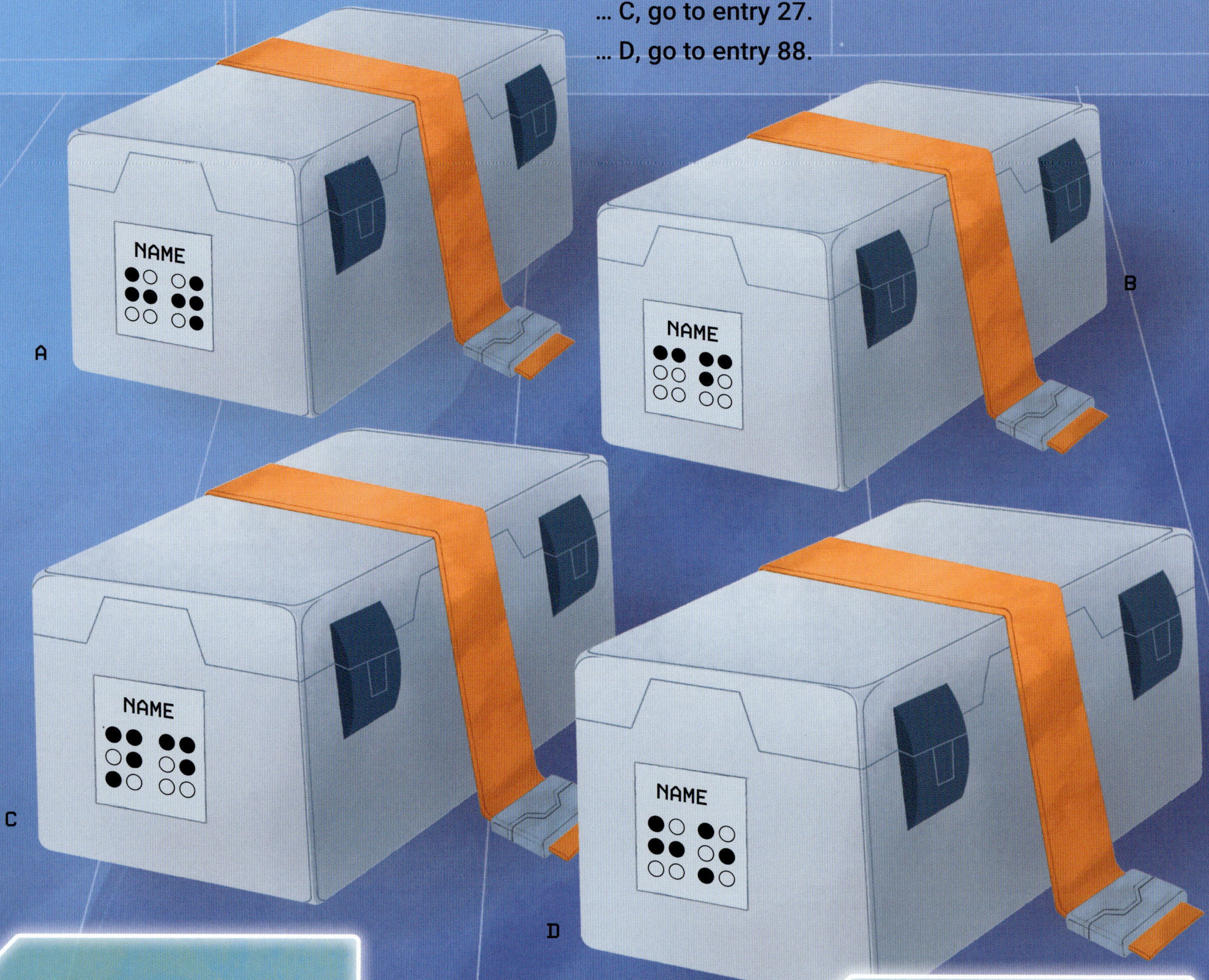

137
That's not the right constellation. Stargaze your way back to entry 82.

138
Those coordinates won't get you to the O.S.L. Navigate back to entry 40.

139
No, you won't find axtris cocoyum there! Head back to entry 174.

140

You managed to rescue your safety tether, but SNIP-P1's saw tore a hole in the O.S.L's hull! You reach into your pocket and pull out a can of fractal freezing foam to seal the tear. It should hold for now, but you know it will melt when the sun rises.

TIP: CHECK OUT THE TIME ON THE CLOCK IN ENTRY 43.

9:33 pm

You realize the sun will rise and melt the sealant in ...

... 59 minutes, go to entry 167.

... 67 minutes, go to entry 63.

... 89 minutes, go to entry 29.

... 56 minutes, go to entry 76.

141
Nope, that docking station isn't compatible. Back up to entry 153.

142
Nope, it wasn't in the air lock. Head back to entry 205.

143

At the medical bay, you meet Dr. Halley Wong, who has just received her supply box from Fox. However, something seems to be missing. She hands you her supply request form, so you can see what she ordered.

You realize that Dr. Wong is missing …

… one tube of dark matter burn cream, go to entry 111.
… one pack of anti-stardust wipes, go to entry 89.
… one bottle of hypersleep essence, go to entry 33.
… one interdimensional travel sickness patch, go to entry 120.

Resupply request form PX1

REQUESTOR: Dr. Halley Wong

Item	Quantity
Dark matter burn cream	3
Hypersleep essence	6
Extra mercury thermometer	7
Pack of anti-stardust wipes	9
Space blanket (large)	4
Emergency chocolate bar	5
Interdimensional travel sickness patch	8
Inner ear equilibrium elixir	6
Cosmic dust eye drops	2
Anti-itch space suit spray	1

AUTHORIZED BY: Commander Nova Darwish

144 I'm afraid that's not the right answer. Make your way back to entry 184.

145 That's not the right constellation. Stargaze your way back to entry 82.

146 That's not the geyser-free route! Take your singed eyebrows back to entry 133.

147

You run to the escape pod to try to intercept Fox. Now that MAL is no longer compromised, things should be smoother, right? Wrong! Fox has managed to reprogram the rest of the helper robots, and as you reach the escape pod, BEN-D1 is waiting for you, holding the door shut. The only way to override BEN-D1 is to answer a number riddle.

> TO GET THE SAME ANSWER TO ALL FOUR EQUATIONS, JUST USE THE BUTTONS—BUT WHICH ONES?

7 ☐ 5
15 ☐ 3
2 ☐ 6
8 ☐ 4

+ − × ÷

You think carefully, then hit the buttons ...

× , ÷ , × , ÷ , go to entry 92.
+ , − , × , + , go to entry 166.
− , ÷ , + , − , go to entry 87

148
That's not the code to open the fuel valve. Head back to entry 57.

149
I'm afraid that's not quite right. Untangle your way back to entry 150.

150

You sprint toward the crew's quarters via the recreation bay, but suddenly, dozens of ventilation tubes spring from the walls like snakes, twisting and writhing their way around you and HAN-D1, pinning you against the side of the access tunnel. MAL's voice crackles through the speakers.

> DID YOU REALLY THINK I'D LET YOU REBOOT ME WITHOUT A FIGHT? LET'S SEE YOU CRACK THIS ONE. MULTIPLY ME BY ANY OTHER NUMBER, AND THE ANSWER WILL ALWAYS BE THE SAME. WHAT NUMBER AM I?

You prise a tube away from your mouth and shout ...

... "One!" go to entry 149.
... "Ten!" go to entry 32.
... "Zero!" go to entry 13.
... "Two!" go to entry 2.

151
You won't make it in time going this way! Sprint back to entry 100.

152
That's not the code to restart the stabilizer. Float back to entry 76, and try again.

153

Your boots are correctly calibrated, and your heart is thumping as you inch ever closer to the O.S.L. The O.S.L. has four docking ports, but your capsule is only compatible with one of them. Choose carefully!

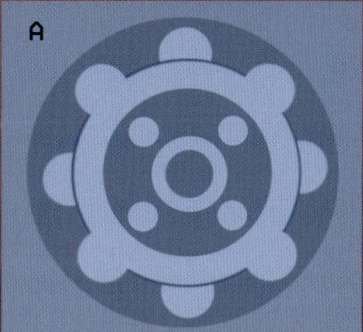
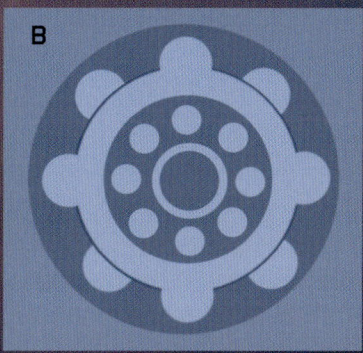
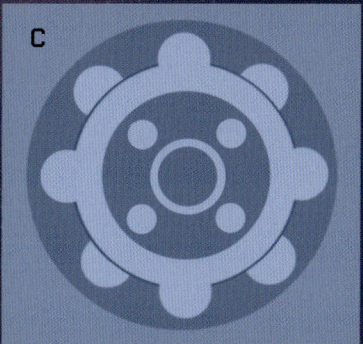
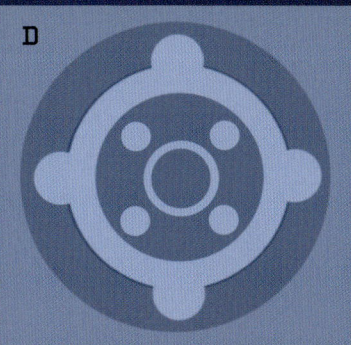

You choose to connect with docking port …
… A, go to entry 141.
… B, go to entry 73.
… C, go to entry 61.
… D, go to entry 102.

154
You won't find the reboot code word in there. Put the book back, and return to entry 53.

155
I'm afraid that's a fake key card. Swipe your way back to entry 16.

156

Good detective work, you're on Klixanovia! HAN-D1 brings you an interplanetary guidebook, which has some helpful Klixanovian phrases. You greet the aliens warmly, explain where you're from, and ask for their help.

LINGUIST'S GUIDE TO THE GALAXY
Chapter 42: Klixanovian

KLIXANOVIAN	ENGLISH
Whump	Poison
Axtris	Stars
Flinflan	Hello
Bik	From
Cocoyum	Chocolate
Zu	You
Bleebo	Goodbye
Yeeyow	Monster
Tse	We

KLIXANOVIAN	ENGLISH
Delipt	Love
Venk	Come
Terak	Earth
Sloon	Please
Tiktak	Thank you
Plitz	Help
Ous	Us
Flerb	Travel
Glerp	Safe

You repeat the phrase ...

... "Bleebo. Tse delipt whump. Flerb glerp," go to entry 10.

... "Flinflan. Tse venk bik Terak. Sloon plitz ous," go to entry 195.

... "Flinflan. Zu venk bik Terak. Tiktak," go to entry 185.

157
That attachment won't fit the release mechanism. Turn back to entry 166.

158
That's not your safety tether. Quick, float back to entry 160 while you still can!

159
That's not the right wire! Nip back to entry 5 to try again.

160

You enter the code, and the hatch lock clunks open. You pull on your suit and make your way out to the stabilizer. The O.S.L. is spinning wildly as it gets slowly pulled toward the black hole, but you hold on tight as you unscrew the cover of the stabilizer. A noise behind you announces the arrival of another hacked robot. SNIP-P1 is going straight for your safety tether! You've got time to pull it out of SNIP-P1's reach, but which one is it?

You reach forward and pull tether …

… A, go to entry 158.
… B, go to entry 140.
… C, go to entry 77.

161
That's not the correct reboot code word. Puzzle your way back to entry 72.

162
You won't find the reboot code word in there. Put the photo back, and return to entry 53.

163 Nice one! Now that you've ruled out jabberon, Science Officer Hoshi Ohsumi shows you the O.S.L.'s state-of-the-art quantum magnifiers. He says they're so powerful that they can see the atomic structure of any matter. You put on the headset, and Ohsumi inserts the samples of pharz and zeplium.

"TO BE A GOOD FUEL SOURCE, THE ELEMENT NEEDS TO HAVE THREE TIMES AS MANY ELECTRONS AS NEUTRONS, TWICE AS MANY PROTONS AS NEUTRONS, AND AN EVEN TOTAL NUMBER OF PROTONS AND NEUTRONS."

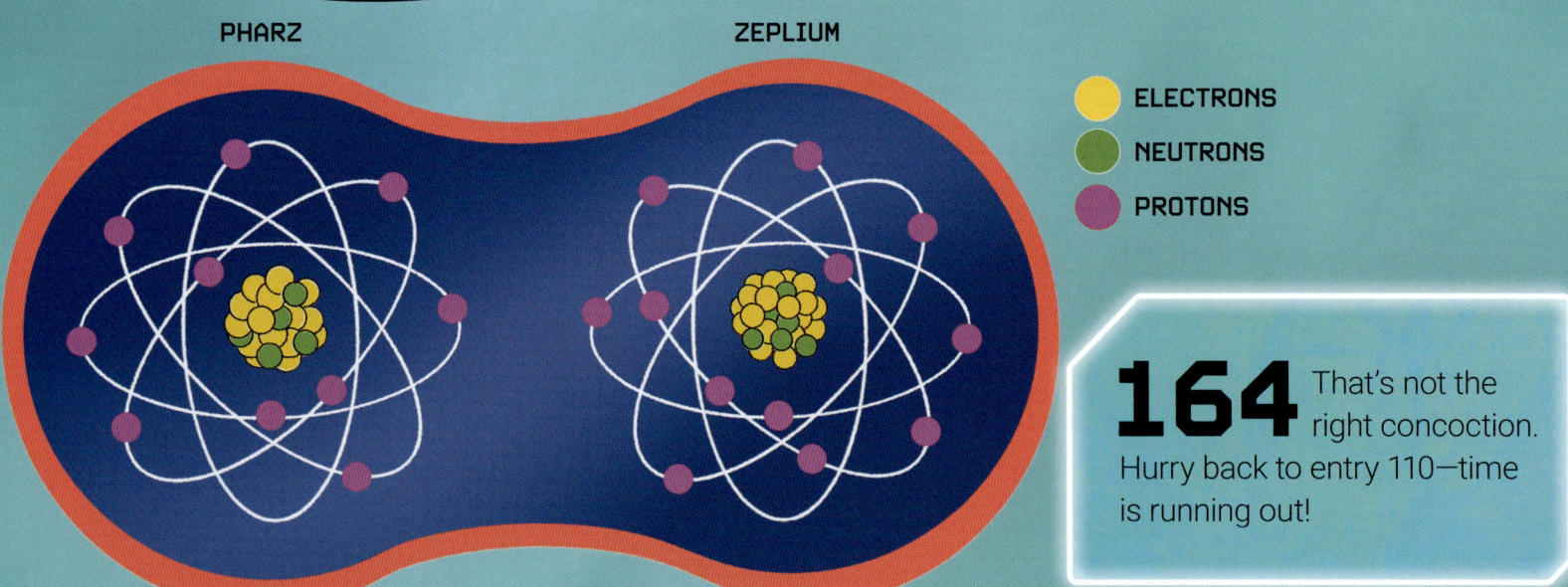

PHARZ ZEPLIUM

● ELECTRONS
● NEUTRONS
● PROTONS

164 That's not the right concoction. Hurry back to entry 110—time is running out!

165 No, you're not on Egnog. Find your way back to entry 47, and try again.

Based on this criteria, you determine that the viable fuel source is …

… neither zeplium nor pharz, go to entry 44.

… zeplium, go to entry 205.

… pharz, go to entry 183.

166

Nice work! BEN-D1 lets you pass, but by the time you reach the escape pod, Fox has already slipped inside. You can't let him leave with the zeplium. If you can disable the release mechanism, you should be able to stop the pod from leaving. Luckily, HAN-D1 has many attachments for just such an occasion!

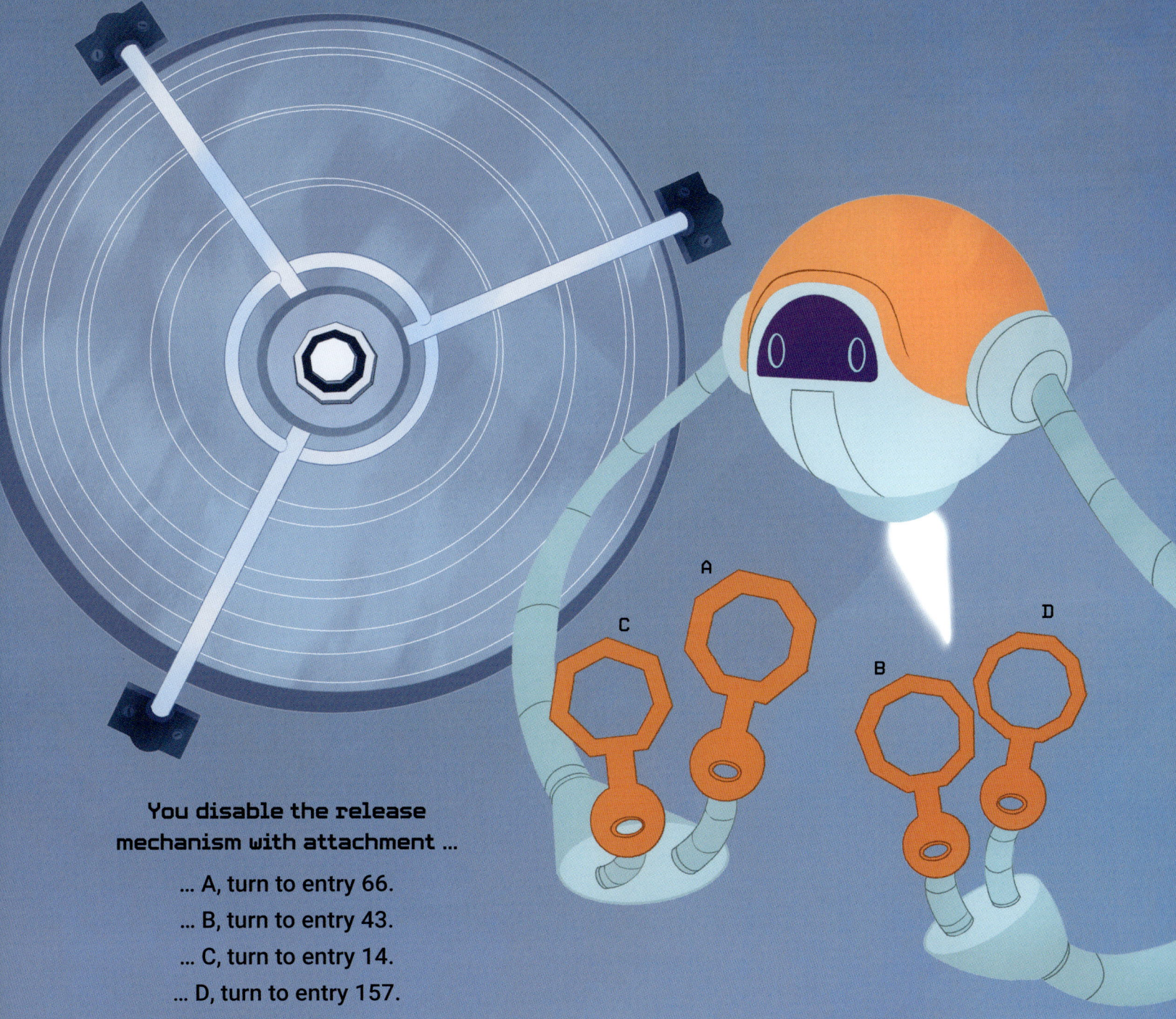

You disable the release mechanism with attachment …

… A, turn to entry 66.
… B, turn to entry 43.
… C, turn to entry 14.
… D, turn to entry 157.

167
No, that's not how long you have until the sun rises. Try again back at entry 140.

168
Oops, that's not the docking probe button! Probe your way back to entry 107.

169
That's not the code name for the manual override. Zip back to entry 187.

170

Now it finally makes sense! Fox wanted to sell the secrets of the O.S.L. to the highest bidder. He hacked MAL and the helper robots and tried to sabotage everything once you'd figured out that zeplium was a viable fuel source. You and the crew head to the escape pod to confront Fox. He's locked himself in, but Commander Darwish has the master code. The only problem is she's still groggy from the hypersleep.

I REMEMBER THAT IT'S AN ODD NUMBER BETWEEN 1 AND 50 AND THAT IT'S A MULTIPLE OF THREE. AND I'M SURE IT'S A SQUARE NUMBER.

You work it out and enter the door code ...

... 9, go to entry 86.
... 21, go to entry 128.
... 25, go to entry 36.
... 36, go to entry 95.

171
That's not quite the right code. Take another look back at entry 65.

172
I'm afraid that's not the robot's passcode. Make your way back to entry 19.

173
No, I'm afraid that's not the right gravity level. Bounce back to entry 180, and try again.

174 The fuel valve clicks open, and you empty your backpack of sparkling zeplium into the tank. Instantly, the O.S.L. starts to rumble to life. You did it! You turn to your guidebook from entry 156 and thank your new Klixanovian friends. You ask them what you can give them in return for their zeplium and their kindness.

TSE DELIPT AxTRIS COCOYUM!

You know you can find exactly what the aliens are after in …

… the lab, go to entry 117.
… Dr. Wong's supply box, go to entry 103.
… Commander Darwish's cabin, go to entry 139.
… the control room, go to entry 42.

175 No, that's not the missing piece. Puzzle your way back to entry 103.

176 That circuit board won't work. Do the robot all the way back to entry 191.

177

Good job, you're on course to the O.S.L. You get ready to sit back and relax, but suddenly the radar starts beeping. You're headed straight into an asteroid belt! There's no way around it, so you'll have to go through it. Hold on tight!

  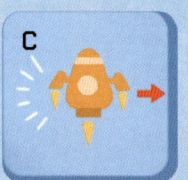 

You know the rear thruster moves you forward, the front thruster moves you backward, the left thruster moves you right, and the right thruster moves you left. You take a deep breath and follow the sequence …

… AACCAADDDBDDBBDAA, go to entry 197.

… AADDBBCCCACCBBDAA, go to entry 18.

… AACCAADDDBDDAACAA, go to entry 107.

178
Nothing good awaits you in this tunnel! Carefully tiptoe back to entry 202.

179
You won't find the entrance to the zeplium mine there. Recalculate and return to entry 79.

180

That's the right code! You hurry back inside as HAL counts down to the emergency wormhole. Then there is an almighty flash. When your eyesight returns to normal, the view through the portholes is completely different. The O.S.L. has jumped through the wormhole to an alien planet! Before you can venture outside, you'll need to set up your boots. MAL calculates that the gravity outside is a third of the gravity on the O.S.L.

You calibrate your gravity boots to level ...

... 6, go to entry 62.
... 3, go to entry 93.
... 1, go to entry 173.

181
That's not the right amount of zeplium. Take your backpack back to entry 114.

182
No, fortunately, you have longer than that. Head straight back to entry 125.

183
I'm afraid that's not correct. Take a closer look back at entry 163.

184

Very impressive! You've correctly identified the four elements, and Science Officer Jericho Nash invites you to examine them under the microscope. He explains that you have to ensure that none of the four elements is in the Intergalactic Unstable Element Directory.

JABBERON

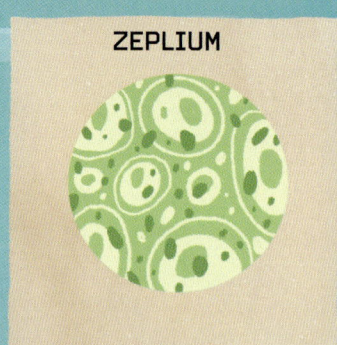
ZEPLIUM

PHARZ

KLERPITE

INTERGALACTIC UNSTABLE ELEMENT DIRECTORY

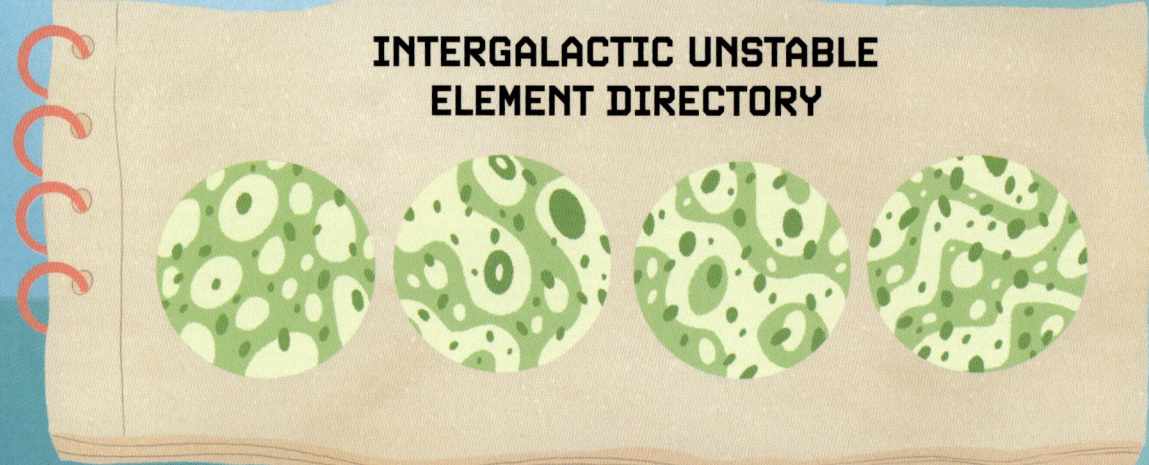

You look carefully and realize ...

... klerpite is in the IUED, go to entry 50.
... none of the elements is in the IUED, go to entry 144.
... zeplium is in the IUED, go to entry 11.
... all of the elements are in the IUED, go to entry 196.

185
Your Klixanovian needs some work! *Flerb* back to entry 156, and try again.

186
That route won't get you there. Retrace your steps back to entry 9.

187

You arrive at the control room in time to input the reboot code, but the countdown continues! Someone must have activated the manual override. You know all the flight systems have code names, but someone has torn up the cheat sheet with the code names on it. Perhaps MAL isn't the only one working against you on the O.S.L. ...

You piece the cheat sheet back together and figure out that the manual override code name is ...

... Pollux, go to entry 64.
... Sirius, go to entry 126.
... Arcturus, go to entry 5.
... Vega, go to entry 169.

188 I'm afraid there's no other route to the crew's quarters. Double back to entry 13.

189 That's not the right calibration for your gravity boots. Float back to entry 27.

190 I'm afraid those aren't the right elements. Check the chart again back at entry 33.

191

The door clicks open. Fox certainly wasn't kidding about MAL acting up. As Fox shows you around the galley, he points out that the station's helper robots that have all mysteriously gone offline. You've always been great at fixing things, so you offer to take a look at one of the robots.

You replace the fried circuit board with part ...

... A, go to entry 55.
... B, go to entry 176.
... C, go to entry 9.

192 I'm afraid that's a fake key card. Swipe your way back to entry 16.

193 No, you definitely do need that part! Put it back carefully, and return to entry 93.

194 That's not the right wire! Nip back to entry 5 to try again.

195 The aliens welcome you and say they've always wanted to meet an Earthling. You explain to them that you need fuel to get the O.S.L. off the ground and back home. They chat excitedly among themselves, then one of them draws a symbol in the sand.

You recognize this symbol from the Intergalactic Table of Elements poster from entry 33. It's the chemical symbol for …

… wiggon, go to entry 101.
… fibblium, go to entry 24.
… zeplium, go to entry 79.
… gorpesium, go to entry 123.

196 That's not quite right, they're not all in the IUED. Make your way back to entry 184.

197 Impact! Impact! Quickly steer back to entry 177.

198 That's right, there's no sign of Fox—or the zeplium sample. That can't be a coincidence. Luckily, MAL is back online—and very apologetic. Determined to help you catch whoever sabotaged its system, MAL shines special infrared lighting on the ground to track Fox's movements. HAN-D1 displays an aerial plan showing the infrared results.

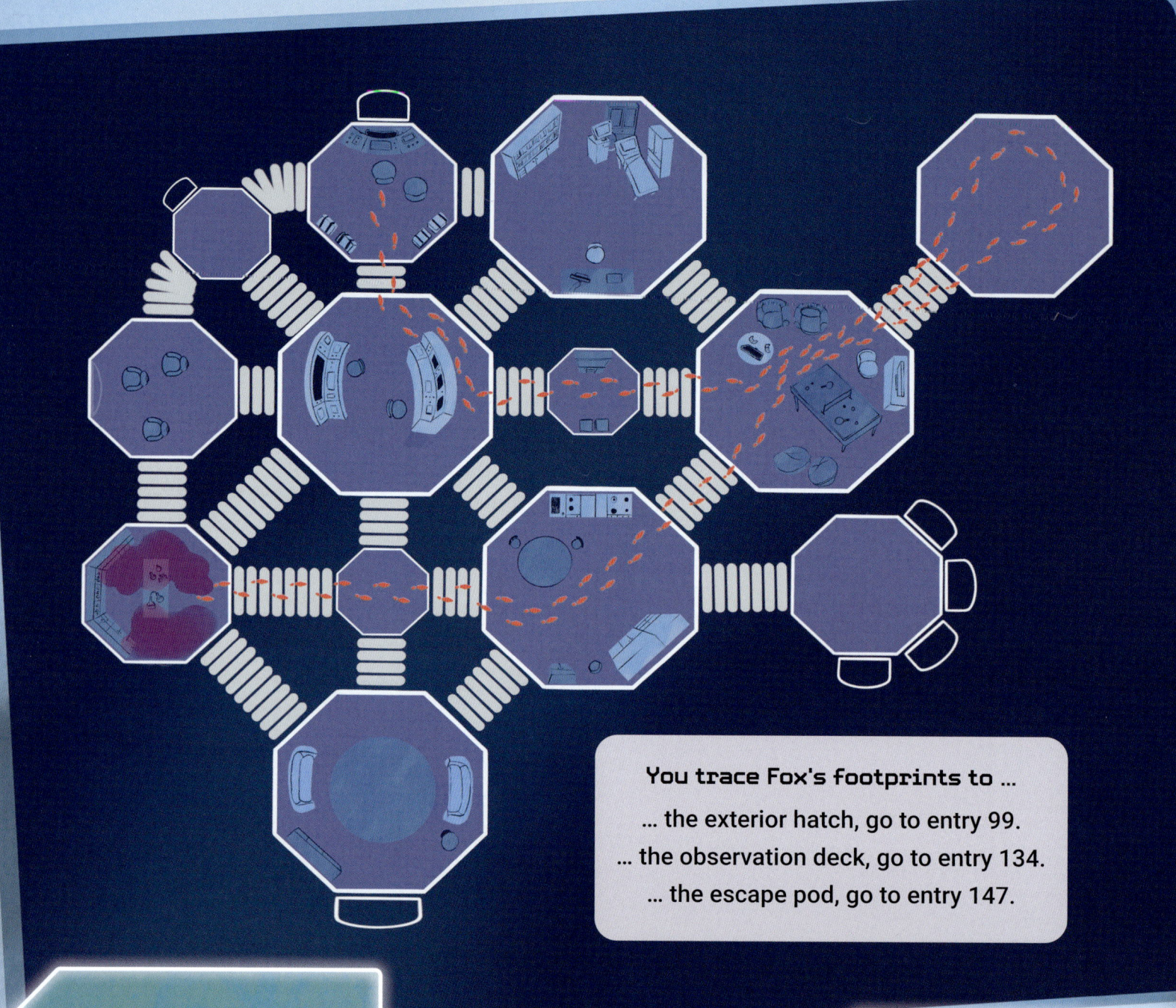

You trace Fox's footprints to ...
... the exterior hatch, go to entry 99.
... the observation deck, go to entry 134.
... the escape pod, go to entry 147.

199 That combination won't open the hatch. Dial your way back to entry 61.

200 That's not the right calibration for your gravity boots. Float back to entry 27.

201 That's not the code to restart the stabilizer. Float back to entry 76, and try again.

202

Phew! You made it through Geyser Grove, but you don't have much time to rest. As soon as you turn the corner, you spot the entrance to the zeplium mine. You made it! The aliens told you that there are three tunnels at the entrance, but only one of them will get you to the zeplium in one piece.

You fold up your map and head into …

… the left-hand tunnel, go to entry 114.
… the middle tunnel, go to entry 178.
… the right-hand tunnel, go to entry 8.

203
That's not the code to open the fuel valve. Head back to entry 57.

204
Those coordinates won't get you to the O.S.L. Navigate back to entry 40.

205

You've done it! You've identified zeplium as the viable fuel source! But before you and the crew can celebrate, an ear-piercing alarm goes off, and a strange purple mist begins to seep out of the ventilation ducts—it's hypersleep essence! Commander Darwish springs into action, pressing a small object into your hand and pushing you out of the lab seconds before the purple cloud engulfs the room.

I don't have time to explain, but this will!

You know you've seen this shape before—it was ...

... in the medical bay, go to entry 4.
... on the helper robot, go to entry 19.
... in the air lock, go to entry 142.

TIP: PERHAPS A CLOSER LOOK AT ENTRY 191 WILL GIVE YOU A CLUE?

206
No, you're not on Pingonia. Find your way back to entry 47, and try again.

207
No, that's not the missing piece. Puzzle your way back to entry 103.

208
Oops, that's not the correct launch sequence. The only place you're going is back to entry 1!